THE REINVENTING GOVERNMENT WORKBOOK

INTRODUCING FRONTLINE EMPLOYEES TO REINVENTION

DAVID OSBORNE

AND

VICTOR COLÓN RIVERA

BASED ON THE BOOK

REINVENTING GOVERNMENT

BY

DAVID OSBORNE

AND

TED GAEBLER

Jossey-Bass Publishers • San Francisco

Jossey-Bass books and products are available through most bookstores. To contact Jossey-Bass directly, call (888) 378-2537, www.josseybass.com.

Substantial discounts on bulk quantities of Jossey-Bass books are available to corporations, professional associations, and other organizations. For details and discount information, contact the special sales department at Jossey-Bass.

For sales outside the United States, please contact your local Simon & Schuster International Office.

ISBN: 0-7879-4100-X

Interior design by Joseph Piliero

Credits are on page 110.

PB Printing 10 9 8 7 6 5 4 3 2 1   FIRST EDITION

CONTENTS

INTRODUCTION

Our governments are in deep trouble today. This book is for those who are disturbed by that reality. It is for those who care about government—because they work in government, or work with government, or study government, or

> *"The basis of effective government is public confidence."*
>
> —JOHN F. KENNEDY

simply want and need their governments to be more effective. It is for those who know something is wrong but are not sure just what it is, for those who have glimpsed a better way, but are not sure just how to bring it to life; for those who have launched successful experiments, but have watched those in power ignore them; for those who have a sense of where government needs to go but are not quite sure how to get there.

REINVENTING GOVERNMENT, P. XV

The Reinventing Government Workbook charts a new course for those who are searching for ways to make our government better. This workbook brings to life the ideas in the book *Reinventing Government* by helping you to:

✔ Understand the ten principles of reinventing government.

✔ Apply these principles to your organization.

In addition, this workbook offers you:

✔ Guidance in developing innovative and better ways of conducting public business.

✔ Tools and techniques you can use to increase the effectiveness of your organization.

✔ Examples of successful governments that are reinventing themselves today. These examples are an excellent source of ideas to jump-start your own organization's reinventing efforts.

Indicate whether each statement is true **(T)** or false **(F)**.

T   F   1. Government is something fixed, something that does not change.

T   F   2. Central control of governmental service is essential for good government.

T   F   3. The word *bureaucracy* connotes a rational, efficient method of organization.

T   F   4. Government should be run like a business.

T   F   5. Our public schools are among the best in the developed world.

T   F   6. The GI Bill was perhaps the most successful social program in American history.

T   F   7. People are more productive when they feel a sense of ownership of their work.

T   F   8. When we say government's "customer" we mean "citizen."

T   F   9. Government is not affected by our information- and knowledge-rich society.

T   F   10. Government does not influence business.

ASSUMPTIONS

Government *is* important. It is the mechanism we use to make communal decisions; it is the way we provide services that benefit all our people; it is the way we solve collective problems.

> *"If men were angels, no government would be necessary."*
>
> —JAMES MADISON (1751–1836)

Civilized society cannot function effectively without effective government.

The people who work in government are not the problem; the *systems* in which they work are the problem.

Neither traditional liberalism nor traditional conservatism has much relevance to the problems our governments face today. We do not need more government or less government, we need *better* government.

Equity—equal opportunity for all citizens—is essential; reinventing government can *increase* that equity.

THE BANKRUPTCY OF BUREAUCRACY

The kind of governments that developed during the industrial era, with their sluggish, centralized bureaucracies, their preoccupation with rules and regulations, and their hierarchical chains of command, no longer work very well. They accomplished great things in their time, but somewhere along the line they got away from us. They became bloated, wasteful, ineffective. And when the world began to change, they failed to change with it. Hierarchical, centralized bureaucracies designed in the 1930s or 1940s simply do not function well in the rapidly changing, information-rich, knowledge-intensive society and economy of the 1990s. They are like luxury ocean liners in an age of supersonic jets: big, cumbersome, expensive, and extremely difficult to turn around. Gradually, new kinds of public institutions are taking their place.

"The greatest mistake citizens can make when they complain of 'the bureaucracy' is to suppose that their frustrations arise simply out of management problems; they do not— they arise out of governance problems."

—JAMES Q. WILSON, BUREAUCRACY

REINVENTING GOVERNMENT, PP. 11–12

PUBLIC INSTITUTIONS

Name at least three large, bureaucratic public institutions created before 1970.

A.

B.

C.

Now, by placing an X on the scale below, rank the three public institutions you have listed above, in terms of productivity and effectiveness.

Poor									*Excellent*
1	2	3	4	5	6	7	8	9	10

A. _____

B. _____

C. _____

> **Between saying and doing many a pair of shoes is worn out.**
>
> —ITALIAN PROVERB

THE EMERGENCE OF ENTREPRENEURIAL GOVERNMENT

We use the phrase entrepreneurial government to describe the new model we see emerging. . . . It was coined by the French economist J. B. Say, around the year 1800. "The entrepreneur," Say wrote, "shifts economic resources out of an area of lower and into an area of higher productivity and greater yield."

REINVENTING GOVERNMENT, P. XIX

According to Thomas Kuhn, author of The Structure of Scientific Revolutions, *a paradigm was a set of assumptions about reality—an accepted model or pattern—that explained the world better than any other set of assumptions.*

By entrepreneurial, in other words, we don't mean "private sector" or "profit seeking." We mean organizations that constantly seek to use their resources in new ways to maximize their productivity and yield. Translated into public sector terms, this means organizations that strive constantly to increase their efficiency and effectiveness.

This is not to say that government should be run like a business. Government and business are fundamentally different institutions, driven by fundamentally different incentives. These incentives include:

♦ Businesses are funded by their customers; most public institutions are funded by legislatures.

♦ Businesses strive for profit; public institutions strive to serve the public.

♦ Business leaders make quick decisions behind closed doors; public leaders make slower decisions through democratic processes.

But government can be more entrepreneurial. . . .

E X E R C I S E 2
NEW PARADIGMS:
GOING BEYOND WHAT IS

A. Using four straight lines, connect the following nine dots—without lifting your pen or pencil from the paper.

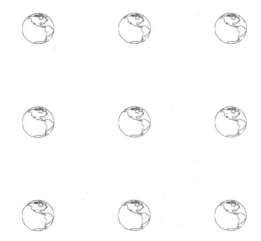

B. Without using a clock or watch, list the ways you would measure the passage of time.

> *"The real voyage of discovery consists not in seeking new lands, but in seeing with new eyes."*
>
> —MARCEL PROUST, QUOTED IN *REINVENTING GOVERNMENT*, P. XXII

EXERCISE 3
PARADIGM SHIFT

By drawing a line, match the new entrepreneurial principle with the old bureaucratic principle it is replacing.

Bureaucratic (From)

Centralized

Rowing

Command-and-Control

Monopolies

Rule-Driven

Process-Oriented

Convenience of Bureaucracy

Focus on Spending

Short-Term, Reactive

Administrative Mechanisms

Entrepreneurial (To)

Mission-Driven

Results-Oriented

Customer-Driven

Anticipatory, Preventive

Decentralized

Steering

Competition

Market Mechanisms

Community Empowerment

Focus on Earning

THE TEN PRINCIPLES OF REINVENTING GOVERNMENT

Module One
Clarifying Your Purpose

I. Customer-Driven Government
II. Mission-Driven Government
III. Anticipatory Government

Module Two
Enhancing Your Performance

IV. Results-Oriented Government
V. Competitive Government
VI. Enterprising Government

Module Four
Increasing Your Leverage

IX. Catalytic Government
X. Market-Oriented Government

Module Three
Shifting Your Locus of Control

VII. Decentralized Government
VIII. Community-Owned Government

MODULE ONE

CLARIFYING YOUR PURPOSE

PRINCIPLE I.

CUSTOMER-DRIVEN GOVERNMENT
MEETING THE NEEDS OF THE CUSTOMER, NOT THE BUREAUCRACY

Democratic governments exist to serve their citizens. Businesses exist to make profits. And yet it is business that searches obsessively for ways to please the . . . people. Few people in government ever use the word

> *"He is well paid that is well satisfied."*
>
> —SHAKESPEARE,
> THE MERCHANT OF VENICE
> (1596–1597)

customer. Most public organizations don't even know who their customers are.

REINVENTING GOVERNMENT, P. 166

Clarifying Your Purpose

The ultimate purpose of most public organizations is customer satisfaction. To achieve that purpose, entrepreneurial governments demand that institutions define their customers, listen to their customers, and give customers choices. These new approaches require that institutions be extremely flexible and adaptable.

On the following scale, indicate to what degree each factor influences the way you provide your service (1 = not at all, 10 = very much).

	1				5					10
1. Funding source	☐	☐	☐	☐	☐	☐	☐	☐	☐	☐
2. Competition	☐	☐	☐	☐	☐	☐	☐	☐	☐	☐
3. Pleasing recipients of service	☐	☐	☐	☐	☐	☐	☐	☐	☐	☐
4. Service complaints/demands	☐	☐	☐	☐	☐	☐	☐	☐	☐	☐
5. Pleasing interest groups	☐	☐	☐	☐	☐	☐	☐	☐	☐	☐
6. Pleasing elected officials	☐	☐	☐	☐	☐	☐	☐	☐	☐	☐
7. Pleasing managers/supervisors	☐	☐	☐	☐	☐	☐	☐	☐	☐	☐
8. Following the rules/regulations	☐	☐	☐	☐	☐	☐	☐	☐	☐	☐
9. Remaining within the job scope	☐	☐	☐	☐	☐	☐	☐	☐	☐	☐
10. Necessity of offering the same service to every customer	☐	☐	☐	☐	☐	☐	☐	☐	☐	☐

> *"When was the last time you felt like a valued customer at your children's school? How about your motor vehicle office? Your city hall?"*
>
> —REINVENTING GOVERNMENT, P. 166

DEFINE YOUR CUSTOMERS

Your primary customers are the individuals or groups that your work is primarily designed to help. Your secondary customers are other individuals or groups that your work is designed to help, but less directly.

EXERCISE 5
EXTERNAL CUSTOMERS

---

1. Who are your primary customers?

2. How many different types of customers does your organization have? Name your secondary customers.

> "A citizen is someone who can express his or her opinion at the ballot box. A customer is a recipient of a specific service: public housing, or job training, or education."
>
> —DAVID OSBORNE,
> "THE POWER OF OUTDATED IDEAS,"
> GOVERNING MAGAZINE, DEC. 1992

3. What customer needs do your services or processes satisfy?

4. What are your customers' quality expectations of your organization?

5. How is your service/process used?

> *"The greatest irritant most people experience in their dealings with government is the arrogance of the bureaucracy. People today expect to be valued as customers—even by government."*
>
> —REINVENTING GOVERNMENT, P. 167

6. Are there alternative services or competitors?

7. What is the frequency of customer use?

8. Where does the customer learn about the service/process?

9. Who actually buys the service/process?

INTERNAL CUSTOMERS

Almost everyone in the organization is a customer of someone else in the organization in that they receive information, service, or another type of support. Meeting these "internal" customers' needs means having these people get the services and information they need efficiently and effectively.

List those within your organization who serve *you* as a customer.

1.

2.

3.

4.

5.

6.

7.

8.

9.

10.

"Everyone has a customer, either inside or outside the organization."

—W. EDWARDS DEMING, "BOARDROOM REPORTS," LESSONS FROM THE MASTER OF MANAGEMENT, MAR. 15, 1994

CUSTOMER VOICE:
LISTENING TO YOUR CUSTOMER

All the management experts, from Peters to Waterman to Drucker and Deming, dwell on the importance of listening to one's customer. They counsel managers to expose their employees directly to their customers.

REINVENTING GOVERNMENT, P. 169

"Give every man thine ear, but few thy voice."

—SHAKESPEARE, HAMLET (1603)

Organizations that truly listen to their customers become customer driven: they restructure their operations around the needs of their customers. They offer customized rather than standardized services.

Example

"The Duval County School Board, in Florida, surveyed its community and discovered a pressing need for day care for latchkey children, before and after school. So the district launched a Community Schools program that keeps most schools open from 7:00 A.M. to 5:45 P.M. School is free, but parents pay $20 a week for the full child-care service."

—*Reinventing Government,* p. 170

**There are dozens of different ways to listen
to the voice of the customer.**

Method	*Example*	*Positive Outcome*
Customer Surveys		
Customer Follow-Up		
Community Surveys		
Customer Contact	Police chief spends one month of every year in the field as frontline officer.	Firsthand information: helpful in policy and strategy decisions.
Customer Contact Reports		
Customer Councils		

Method	Example	Positive Outcome
Focus Groups		
Customer Interviews		
E-Mail		
Customer Service Training		
Test Marketing		
Quality Guarantees		

I hear and I forget;
I see and I remember;
I do and I understand.

Method	Example	Positive Outcome
Inspectors		
Ombudsmen		
Complaint Tracking Systems		
800 Numbers		
Suggestion Boxes or Forms		

> "The reason why we have two ears and only one mouth is that we may listen the more and talk the less."
>
> —ZENO OF CITIUM (C. 300 B.C.)

CUSTOMER CHOICE

The single best way to make public service providers respond to the needs of their customers is to put resources in the customers' hands and let them choose. All the listening techniques listed [previously] are important, but if

the customers do not have a choice of providers—schools, training programs, motor vehicle offices—they remain dependent on the goodwill of the provider.

REINVENTING GOVERNMENT, P. 180

EXERCISE 8
CUSTOMER-DRIVEN: TRUE OR FALSE?

T F **1.** Customer-driven systems force service providers to be accountable to their customers.

T F **2.** Customer-driven systems depoliticize the choice-of-provider decision.

T F **3.** Customer-driven systems stimulate more innovation.

T F **4.** Customer-driven systems give people choices among different kinds of services.

T F **5.** Customer-driven systems empower customers to make choices, and empowered customers are more committed customers.

T F **6.** Customer-driven systems create greater opportunities for equity.

Develop and write possible outcomes for the following scenarios:

1. If public schools were paid a set fee for every child who attended, if parents could choose any public school, and if any group or organization could seek a charter to create a new public school, how would principals and teachers respond?

2. If motor vehicle offices were paid a set fee for each transaction they processed, if customers could do business at any location, and if any business could seek a charter to open motor vehicle offices, how would government motor vehicle offices change?

Circle the item or items that put resources in the customers' hands.

Clue: Vouchers, cash grants, set $ amount to customer

Food stamps	Pell grants	Most higher education systems
Veterans' hospitals	GI Bill	Mortgage interest tax deduction
Motor vehicle department	Public works	Public education

> *"Public agencies get most of their funding from legislatures, city councils, and elected boards. And most of their 'customers' are captive: short of moving, they have few alternatives to the services their governments provide. So managers in the public sector learn to ignore them."*
>
> —REINVENTING GOVERNMENT, P. 167

ADVANTAGES OF CUSTOMER-DRIVEN SYSTEMS

1.

2.

3.

4.

5.

6.

CUSTOMIZED SERVICES

List services that are customized to your particular style and taste and indicate their corresponding sector by placing a check mark in the appropriate column.

Waiting Long?

	List Service	Private Sector	Public Sector
1.		✔	✔
2.			
3.			
4.			
5.			
6.			

> *"In a world in which cable television systems have 50 channels, banks let their customers do business by phone, and even department stores have begun to customize their services for the individual, bureaucratic, unresponsive, one-size-fits-all government cannot last."*
>
> —*REINVENTING GOVERNMENT*, P. 194

RESTRUCTURING WORK PROCESSES TO ADD VALUE FOR YOUR CUSTOMERS: THE TOTAL QUALITY METHOD

[Total Quality Management is a philosophy developed principally by W. Edwards Deming.] *Deming's approach uses performance data to pinpoint problems, then gives employees tools they can use to analyze them, isolate their root causes, develop solutions, and implement them.*

REINVENTING GOVERNMENT, PP. 159–160

> *"85 percent of problems can only be corrected by changing the systems . . . and less than 15 percent are under a worker's control."*
>
> —PETER R. SCHOLTES,
> THE TEAM HANDBOOK, PP. 2–8

Quality Management

♦ Make decisions based on data rather than on hunches or intuition.

♦ Look for root causes of problems rather than reacting to superficial symptoms.

♦ Seek permanent solutions rather than quick fixes.

♦ Empower and train people who perform the job to solve the problem.

♦ Use teams.

Organizations should be seen as systems designed to serve the customer. Your customers are those who benefit from your work. They can best determine what quality is; they can tell you what they want and how they want it.

Customers are the most important people to an organization: *work backwards from there.* Those who serve customers directly are next; management is there to serve those who serve customers. *Key:* Constantly ask customers what they want, then shape the entire service and production processes to produce it. *Ask:* How does this add value for the customer?

Tips

1. Require systemic culture change. Create a culture of continuous improvement.

2. Avoid applying quality techniques only to isolated systems or programs. Focus on the big systems as well as the small: budget, personnel, procurement, planning, and auditing.

3. Instill continuous learning. Everyone is responsible for improving the product or service, and should be empowered to do so.

4. Measure both performance and process. Define success in terms of how well "customers" are served. Emphasize goals, standards, and continuous improvement.

5. Recognize that the quality process takes time. Bringing quality management to government is tougher than bringing it to business. *Reason:* There are many more stakeholders with conflicting desires and interests.

MISSION-DRIVEN GOVERNMENT
TRANSFORMING RULE-DRIVEN ORGANIZATIONS

At the core of an organization is its purpose or mission. The mission provides the guiding direction for developing strategy, defining critical success factors, searching out key opportunities, making resource allocation choices and pleasing customers . . . The mission is the synthesis of what the customers see as your service, what employees in your group see as its service, what your product or service should be, who your customers are and what value you bring to them.

> **"Never tell people how to do things. Tell them what you want them to achieve and they will surprise you with their ingenuity."**
>
> —GENERAL GEORGE S. PATTON (1885–1945)

—C. D. SCOTT, D. T. JAFFE, AND G. R. TOBE, ORGANIZATIONAL VISION, VALUES, AND MISSION, P. 62

Clarifying Your Purpose

Entrepreneurial governments clarify their missions, then scrape off the excess rules, regulations, and obsolete activities that get in the way.

A Word on Rules and Regulations

We embrace our rules and red tape to prevent bad things from happening, of course. But those same rules prevent good things from happening. They slow government to a snail's pace. They make it impossible to respond to rapidly changing environments. They build wasted time and effort into the very fabric of the organization.

REINVENTING GOVERNMENT, P. 111

Consider this:

☞ The Lord's Prayer has 56 words.

☞ The 23rd Psalm has 118 words.

☞ The Gettysburg Address has 226 words.

☞ The Ten Commandments have 297 words.

☞ A USDA order on the price of cabbage has 15,629 words.

CLARIFYING YOUR MISSION: CREATE A MISSION STATEMENT

A mission statement articulates the fundamental purpose of the organization. It is a guiding tool that drives the organization.

☞ Everyone in the organization gets clear about the fundamental purpose of their work.

☞ Management eliminates obsolete or conflicting missions.

☞ Employees make decisions and know what course of action to take.

☞ Customers understand what you offer, how, and what value you bring to them.

CHUNKING AND HIVING

> ***Chunking:*** Breaking up large organizations into small groups, each with a clear mission
>
> ***Hiving:*** Spinning off new teams and organizations

Most public institutions have been designed to serve mass markets—for example, the schools have been designed to educate all children, the U.S. Postal Service has been designed to deliver all mail. However, institutions often work better when their mission is to serve *one* niche.

WRITE YOUR PERSONAL MISSION STATEMENT

_____

_____

_____

_____

_____

> "Our mission is to:
> - **Provide the world's best combat air forces.**
> - **Deliver rapid, decisive air power anytime, anywhere."**
>
> —AIR COMBAT COMMAND

WRITE YOUR ORGANIZATIONAL MISSION STATEMENT

_____

_____

_____

_____

_____

> "Working together to:
> - **Provide leadership**
> - **Create partnerships**
> - **Build neighborhoods**
> - **Strengthen business**
> - **Deliver quality services**
> - **Reduce the cost of government."**
>
> —MISSION OF HARTFORD CITY GOVERNMENT

ORGANIZING BY MISSION
RATHER THAN BY TURF

Missions do not respect turf lines. *Problem:* Organizations built around turf rather than mission tend to be schizophrenic.

> *"If a rat is found in an apartment, it is a housing inspection responsibility; if it runs into a restaurant, the health department has jurisdiction; if it goes outside and dies in an alley, public works takes over."*
>
> —JOHN MUDD,
> NEIGHBORHOOD SERVICES

EXERCISE 12
MISSION VS. TURF

Give examples of *turf-driven* and *mission-driven* organizations:

Turf-Driven Organization	Mission-Driven Organization

THE ADVANTAGES
OF MISSION-DRIVEN
GOVERNMENT

Mission-Driven Organizations	Examples
• More efficient than rule-driven organizations	
• More effective than rule-driven organizations	
• More innovative than rule-driven organizations	
• More flexible than rule-driven organizations	
• Have higher morale than rule-driven organizations	

Create a Culture
Around the Mission

"To imprint the mission of an organization on its members, leaders build a culture around it. They articulate their values and model the behavior they want."

—*REINVENTING GOVERNMENT*, P. 132

REMOVING THE OBSTACLES TO THE ACCOMPLISHMENT OF YOUR MISSION

The first step is to scrape off the barnacles of obsolete rules and activities. Government's rules are aggregated into systems:

1. Budget systems

2. Personnel systems

3. Purchasing systems

4. Accounting systems

5. Auditing systems

---

1. Budget Systems

Most public budgets fence agency money into dozens of separate accounts, often called *line items. Reason:* to control the bureaucrats. *Solution:* a mission-driven budget, which empowers the organization to pursue its mission unencumbered by yesterday's line items.

E X E R C I S E   1 4
MISSION-DRIVEN
BUDGETS

Fill in the boxes with the three basic elements of mission-driven budgets.

A.

B.

C.

EXAMPLES OF MISSION-DRIVEN BUDGETS

Examples	Notes
1. Fairfield, California	
2. Visalia, California	
3. U.S. Forest Service: Eastern Region	
4. Florida State Government	
5. Chesterfield County, Virginia	
6. U.S. Department of Defense Unified Budget Test	

THE STRENGTHS OF MISSION-DRIVEN BUDGETING

Take Notes

In the space provided, list the different ways that mission-driven budgets help organizations to pursue their missions:

> *"Now the dynamics [have] changed. 'Spend it or lose it' gave way to 'save it and invest it.'"*
>
> —*REINVENTING GOVERNMENT*, P. 120

1. _____

_____

2. _____

_____

3. _____

_____

4. _____

_____

5. _____

_____

6. _____

_____

7. _____

_____

2. Personnel Systems

Most personnel systems in American government are derivatives of the federal Civil Service Act of 1883, passed after a disappointed job seeker assassinated President Garfield. A typical Progressive reform, civil service was a well-intended effort to control

> **"The only thing more destructive than a line-item budget system is a personnel system built around civil service."**
>
> —REINVENTING GOVERNMENT, P. 124

specific abuses: patronage hiring and political manipulation of public employees. . . . In business, personnel is a support function, to help managers manage more effectively. In government it is a control

function. . . . Civil service rules are so complex that most managers find them impenetrable.

REINVENTING GOVERNMENT, PP. 124–125

E X E R C I S E   1 5
HIRING

If you were to recruit and hire an employee, what steps would you take?

_____

_____

_____

_____

_____

_____

PERSONNEL SYSTEMS

How do human resource practices in a government bureaucracy compare to those in an entrepreneurial government?

Take Notes

Action	Government Bureaucracy	Entrepreneurial Government
Hiring	Hire most employees from lists of those who have taken written civil service exams—regardless of whether they are motivated or otherwise qualified.	
Classification	Civil service jobs are classified on a graded scale, and pay within each classification is determined by longevity, not by performance.	
Promotion	Promotions are controlled by the personnel department, not by the manager.	
Firing	Time-consuming process; instead, managers tolerate incompetents, transfer them or bump them upstairs.	
Laying Off	Civil service employees with seniority can bump those with lesser seniority. Typically, layoffs comb out the young, eager employees and leave behind the deadwood—in jobs they neither know nor want.	

> ***Creating Permission to Fail***
>
> ***Entrepreneurs are people who fail many times: "If a department or program director does not have the opportunity to do things wrong, authority is lacking to do them right."***
>
> ***—FLORIDA'S STATE MANAGEMENT GUIDE***

ANTICIPATORY GOVERNMENT
PREVENTION RATHER THAN CURE

Traditional bureaucratic governments focus on supplying services to combat problems. . . . There was a time when our governments focused more on prevention: on building water and sewer systems, to prevent disease; on enacting building codes, to prevent fires; on inspecting milk, meat, and restaurants, to prevent illness; on research that would lead to vaccines and other medical cures, to stamp out disease. But as they developed more capacity to deliver services, their attention shifted.

REINVENTING GOVERNMENT, P. 219

Clarifying Your Purpose

Build foresight into your decision making, and whenever possible redefine your purpose as the prevention of problems rather than as the delivery of services.

Examples

✔ **Oregon** has created statewide goals called "Oregon Benchmarks" and a steering council called The Oregon Progress Board to encourage the community to reach those goals.

✔ **Dallas, Texas,** and many other cities have created futures commissions.

✔ **Sunnyvale, California,** projects all revenues and costs, in both its operating and capital budgets, over the next ten years.

✔ **Scottsdale, Arizona,** requires sprinkler systems to be installed in every new building constructed.

✔ Ten states have passed mandatory bottle deposit laws.

GOVERNING WITH FORESIGHT:
ANTICIPATING THE FUTURE

Our ship of state is like a massive ocean liner, with all the luxuries above deck but no radar, no navigation systems, and no preventive maintenance below.

REINVENTING GOVERNMENT, P. 221

E X E R C I S E   1 6
FUTURES

Match the process with its definition by drawing a line between the two.

Futures Commissions	A process of examining an organization's or community's current situation and future trajectory, setting goals, developing a strategy to achieve these goals, and measuring the results.
Strategic Planning	A process through which citizens analyze trends, develop alternative scenarios of the future, and establish goals and recommendations for the community.

"Some governments are not only trying to prevent problems, they are working to anticipate the future—to give themselves radar."

—REINVENTING GOVERNMENT, P. 229

PREVENTION

The bureaucratic model brought with it a preoccupation with service delivery—with rowing. . . . Hence we spend enormous amounts treating symptoms—with more police, more jails, more welfare payments, and higher Medicaid outlays—while prevention strategies go begging.

REINVENTING GOVERNMENT, P. 220

EXERCISE 17
PREVENTION

Develop prevention strategies for the following scenario. Think of a bottom-line reason for the change, look around for something already existing that is similar, and make an action plan.

> You live on a tropical island that has a serious water shortage. The population, which is still growing, has tripled in the last twenty years, and residential complexes are mushrooming. The water system (public reservoirs, public wells, and so forth), built thirty years ago, has not been upgraded and can no longer meet the demand. Water quality is poor. Rainfall is abundant. How would you have prevented this from happening, and what actions would you recommend to tackle the current problem?

MODULE TWO

ENHANCING YOUR PERFORMANCE

PRINCIPLE IV. **RESULTS-ORIENTED GOVERNMENT**

PRINCIPLE V. **COMPETITIVE GOVERNMENT**

PRINCIPLE VI. **ENTERPRISING GOVERNMENT**

RESULTS-ORIENTED GOVERNMENT
BUYING OUTCOMES RATHER THAN INPUTS

Traditional bureaucratic governments . . . focus on inputs, not outcomes. They fund schools based on how many children enroll; welfare based on how many poor people are eligible; police departments based on police estimates of manpower needed to fight crime. . . . It doesn't matter how well the children

> *"Outcomes are often uncertain, delayed, and controversial; procedures are known, immediate, and defined by law or rule."*
>
> —JAMES Q. WILSON, *BUREAUCRACY*, P. 131

do in one school versus another, how many poor people get off welfare into stable jobs, how much the crime rate falls or how secure the public feels.

REINVENTING GOVERNMENT, P. 139

Enhancing Your Performance

Set performance targets, measure the results, and reward those who hit the targets.

Example

"Six states are testing performance standards for entire courts.... They use customer surveys, focus groups, analysis of case files, and other methods to measure things like how accessible the courts are, how affordable justice is, how swiftly courts handle cases, how impartial court decisions are, and how effective courts are in enforcing their orders."

—Reinventing Government, p. 142

Match each word with its correct definition by drawing a line between the two.

| Process | | What the workers do on a day-to-day basis; the work the public entity does. |

| Inputs | | Dollars spent, number of employees used, and time invested in a particular function. |

| Efficiency | | The results of the public entity's work; how the society, the environment, the world changes because of the work. |

| Effectiveness | | A measure of the volume of something actually produced. |

| Cost-Effectiveness | | A measure of how much each unit of output costs. |

| Outputs | | A measure of the quality of output: how well it achieved the desired outcome. |

| Outcomes | | A measure of the cost of each unit of outcome. |

THE POWER OF PERFORMANCE MEASURES

Organizations that measure the results of their work . . . find that the information transforms them.

REINVENTING GOVERNMENT, P. 146

Take Notes

Advantages of Measurement	Example
1. What gets measured gets done.	
2. If you don't measure results, you can't tell success from failure.	
3. If you can't see success, you can't reward it.	
4. If you can't reward success, you're probably rewarding failure.	
5. If you can't see success, you can't learn from it.	
6. If you can't recognize failure, you can't correct it.	
7. If you can demonstrate results, you can win public support.	

ENHANCING PERFORMANCE

How would you enhance performance in the following scenarios? What would you change? What would be the result?

1. The city council has funded $1 million in highway construction. The department of public works has specified the inputs it expects from contractors: so many inches of material A topped by so many inches of material B.

2. A community district funds its schools based on how many students are enrolled in each school.

PUTTING PERFORMANCE MEASURES TO WORK

There are several common ways that governments use performance information to improve their performance. *Best:* use as many as apply to each agency or function.

Take Notes

Approach	Incentives	Examples and Results
1. Paying for performance	Financial incentives: Merit or bonus systems for high-performing individuals, groups, and/or teams.	
2. Managing for performance	While using performance pay and other rewards, also empower employees to use performance data to change their systems and work processes.	
3. Performance-based budgeting	a. Add output and/or outcome measures to a mission-driven budget.	
	b. Budget for service level desired: $X per output or outcome.	
4. Customer-driven budgeting	Put money in customers' hands, and force service providers to earn their keep by pleasing customers.	

PERFORMANCE-BASED BUDGETS

Take Notes

✍ **Sunnyvale, California**

✍ **United States:** *Government Performance and Results Act*

✍ **New Zealand:** *Output Budgeting*

PRINCIPLE V.

COMPETITIVE GOVERNMENT
INJECTING COMPETITION INTO SERVICE DELIVERY

When service providers must compete, they keep their costs down, respond quickly to changing demands, and strive mightily to satisfy their customers. No institution welcomes competition. But while most of us would prefer a comfortable monopoly, competition drives us to embrace innovation and strive for excellence.

> *"The issue is not public versus private. It is competition versus monopoly."*
>
> —JOHN MOFFITT,
> FORMER CHIEF SECRETARY
> TO MASSACHUSETTS GOVERNOR
> WILLIAM WELD,
> *REINVENTING GOVERNMENT*, P. 76

REINVENTING GOVERNMENT, P. 79

Enhancing Your Performance

Use competition to drive improvement.

Example

"Phoenix has used competition not only in garbage collection but in landfill operation, custodial services, parking lot management, golf course management, street sweeping, street repair, food and beverage concessions, printing, and security.... The city auditor estimates savings of $20 million over the first decade...."

—*Reinventing Government, p. 78*

COMPETITION:
TRUE OR FALSE?

Indicate whether each statement is true **(T)** or false **(F)**.

T   F   1. Competition between teams—between organizations—builds morale and encourages creativity.

T   F   2. In most cases, private firms deliver services more economically than public organizations.

T   F   3. Where public and private organizations (of similar size) function in the same marketplace—such as in health care and electrical utilities—their costs and quality are roughly the same.

T   F   4. Where private service providers do not have to compete, they are just as inefficient as public monopolies.

T   F   5. Public monopolies that are thrust fully into competition have little choice but to please their customers.

T   F   6. Governments should use competition in policymaking and regulatory activities.

T   F   7. Once public employees find themselves in competition, they usually enjoy it—if their job security is not at stake.

THE ADVANTAGES
OF COMPETITION

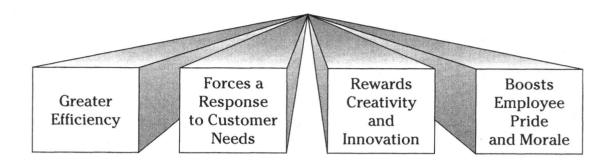

Take Notes

> *"A horse never runs so fast as when he has other horses to catch up with and outpace."*
>
> —Ovid, THE ART OF LOVE (C. A.D. 8), 3, TRANS. J. LEWIS MAY

How would *you* enhance performance and insure positive outcomes?

1. A state relies on private companies to provide automobile insurance. The companies' prices are set by a regulatory commission: every company must charge the same price. The state has found that it has the highest premium rate in the country, the highest claims frequency, and the highest auto theft rate.

2. A city council has voted to contract out garbage collection to the private sector. It has divided the city into five districts and will bid out each one on a five-year contract. The union has protested and public works employees are concerned that they will suffer under this new strategy.

VARIETIES
OF COMPETITION

Public versus Private

1. _____

2. _____

Private versus Private

1. _____

2. _____

Public versus Public

1. _____

2. _____

EXAMPLES OF COMPETITION

> *"Competition is the permanent force for innovation that government normally lacks."*
> —REINVENTING GOVERNMENT, P. 92

Take Notes

Examples	Notes
1. Minnesota's Department of Administration: *Enterprise Management*	
2. East Harlem, *District 4*	
3. *Minnesota School Choice*	

MANAGING COMPETITION: PITFALLS TO AVOID

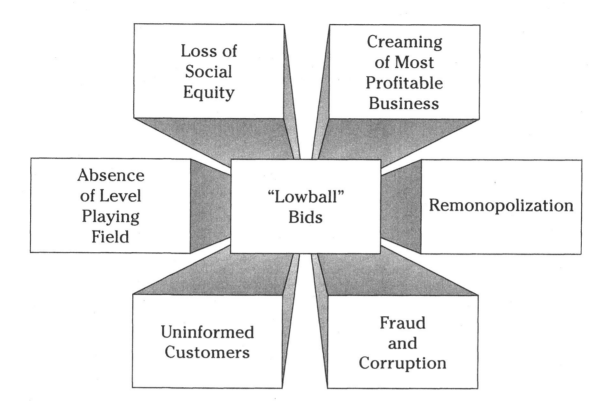

Loss of Social Equity

Creaming of Most Profitable Business

Absence of Level Playing Field

"Lowball" Bids

Remonopolization

Uninformed Customers

Fraud and Corruption

> *"Mixing of social classes and races is extremely important in a democracy; without it, we lose our capacity to understand and empathize with those who are different from us. . . . We become a collection of individuals, not a community."*
> —*REINVENTING GOVERNMENT,* P. 101

PRINCIPLE VI.

ENTERPRISING GOVERNMENT
EARNING RATHER THAN SPENDING

Bottom line: Our public budget systems drive people to spend money, not to earn it. And our employees oblige. Entrepreneurial governments search for non-tax revenues and measure their return on investment. Some even run for-profit enterprises.

REINVENTING GOVERNMENT, PP. 195–196

> *"Getting money is like digging with a needle. Spending it is like water soaking into sand."*
>
> —JAPANESE PROVERB

Enhancing Your Performance

Can you better achieve your mission if you put energy into raising money rather than simply spending it?

ENTERPRISING
GOVERNMENTS

What are the *three basic characteristics* of enterprising governments? Please fill in the boxes:

1.

2.

3.

PROFIT MOTIVE—TURNING IT TO PUBLIC USE: TODAY'S EXAMPLES

Take Notes

Visalia, California, *Recreational Softball:*

Fairfield, California, *Mall and Golf Course:*

Orlando, Florida, *City Hall:*

Milwaukee, Wisconsin, *Metropolitan Sewerage District:*

Phoenix, Arizona, *Waste Water Treatment Plant:*

Chicago, Illinois, *Abandoned Cars:*

Washington State, *Ferry System:*

Paulding County, Georgia, *Prison:*

California, *Enterprising Police Departments:*

> *"Governments look only at the spending side of the ledger. Ignoring returns, they concentrate only on minimizing costs."*
>
> —*REINVENTING GOVERNMENT*, P. 205

CHARGING FEES—RAISING MONEY: TODAY'S EXAMPLES

Perhaps the safest way to raise nontax revenue is simply to charge fees to those who use public services.

REINVENTING GOVERNMENT, P. 203

Advantages: Raise money and lower demand for public services. Both help balance public budgets. *Caution:* Be careful not to exclude the poor from basic services. Provide vouchers or free entry to low-income people if necessary to ensure equity.

> *"All of our public opinion polls indicate that when you confront citizens with their preference for raising revenue—user fees, property tax, local sales tax, local income tax—user fees win hands down."*
>
> —JOHN SHANNON,
> ADVISORY COMMISSION ON
> INTERGOVERNMENTAL RELATIONS

EXERCISE 23
SERVICE FEES

List some services for which governments charge fees:

1.

2.

3.

4.

5.

INVESTING: SPENDING MONEY
TO SAVE MONEY

Businesses focus on both sides of the balance sheet: spending and earning, debits and credits. They don't care as much about the spending side as the earning side:

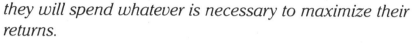

they will spend whatever is necessary to maximize their returns.

REINVENTING GOVERNMENT, P. 205

E X E R C I S E 2 4
INVESTING

Choose either true **(T)** or false **(F)**:

T F Governments normally look only at the spending side of the ledger.

T F Governments normally ignore financial returns, concentrating only on minimizing costs.

T F Governments frequently refuse to consider significant investments that would generate significant returns—simply because of the cost.

INVESTING FOR A RETURN:
TODAY'S EXAMPLES

Take Notes

Santa Clara, California, *Amusement Park:*

Kansas, *Venture Capital Tax Credit:*

Iowa, *Customized Job Training Program:*

TURNING MANAGERS INTO ENTREPRENEURS

If managers cannot keep any of their earnings, they are not likely to pursue them. If managers' budgets are supplied regardless of whether their departments earn anything, they are not likely to spend time trying to make money.

REINVENTING GOVERNMENT, P. 209

Solution: Provide incentives.

Take Notes

Incentives	Notes
Shared savings and earnings	
Innovation capital	
Enterprise funds	
Profit centers	
Identifying the true cost of services	

SHIFTING YOUR LOCUS OF CONTROL

PRINCIPLE VII. **DECENTRALIZED GOVERNMENT**

PRINCIPLE VIII. **COMMUNITY-OWNED GOVERNMENT**

PRINCIPLE VII.

DECENTRALIZED GOVERNMENT
FROM HIERARCHY TO PARTICIPATION AND TEAMWORK

Fifty years ago centralized institutions were indispensable. Information technologies were primitive, communication between different locations was slow, and the public workforce was relatively uneducated.... But today information is virtually limitless, communication between remote locations is instantaneous, many public employees are well educated, and conditions change with blinding speed. There is no time to wait for information to go up the chain of command and decisions to come down.

REINVENTING GOVERNMENT, P. 250

Shifting Your Locus of Control

Stimulate innovation by empowering employees, agencies, and lower levels of government.

"There are lots of people just waiting for you to give them some responsibility, some sense of ownership, something they can take personal pride in. And it's amazing how, once you take those first steps, suddenly a thousand flowers bloom, and the organization takes off in ways that nobody could have predicted."

—GENERAL BILL CREECH,
QUOTED IN *REINVENTING GOVERNMENT*, P. 258

CENTRALIZED CONTROL

In times of crisis traditional leaders instinctively consolidate agencies and centralize controls.

But this instinct increasingly leads to failure. Centralized controls and consolidated agencies generate more waste, not less. . . . Entrepreneurial leaders instinctively reach for the decentralized approach. They move many decisions to "the periphery," . . . into the hands of customers, communities, and nongovernmental organizations. They push others "down below," by flattening hierarchies and giving authority to their employees.

REINVENTING GOVERNMENT, PP. 251–252

ADVANTAGES OF DECENTRALIZED INSTITUTIONS

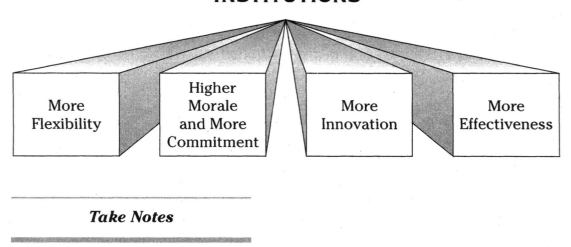

More Flexibility

Higher Morale and More Commitment

More Innovation

More Effectiveness

Take Notes

FOUR METHODS TO HELP SHIFT YOUR LOCUS OF CONTROL

Take Notes

To return control to those who work where the rubber meets the road, entrepreneurial leaders use a variety of methods. These include:

Method 1:

Method 2:

Method 3:

Method 4:

Method Not!

METHOD 1: PARTICIPATORY MANAGEMENT

KEY FACTORS

Take Notes

Approaches	Examples	
1. Labor-management cooperation		
2. No-layoff policies		
3. Flattening the organizational hierarchy		

Example

Ronald Contino used participatory management to turn around the New York City Sanitation Department's Bureau of Motor Equipment. He tapped the ideas of his employees through labor-management committees; handed day-to-day control over operations to line employees; allowed auto mechanics to help write all specifications for new orders, test all new equipment, and staff the unit that negotiated and enforced warranties; and created a Research and Development Group composed entirely of auto mechanics. *Results:* put 85 percent of the garbage trucks back in operation; saved more than $16 million through departmental innovations; implemented at least 50 design improvements and licensed several to private companies, earning royalties for the city.

VARIETIES AND TECHNIQUES OF PARTICIPATORY MANAGEMENT

	Varieties and Techniques	Take Notes
	Quality Circles	
	Labor-Management Committees	
	Employee Development Programs	
	Attitude Surveys	
	Employee Evaluations of Managers	
	Invention Policies	
	Innovation Champions	
	Reward Programs	

METHOD 2: TEAMWORK

Innovative organizations foster constant communication, so information flows quickly through the ranks. To do this, they regularly create new teams and new configurations, so nearly everyone comes into contact with nearly everyone else.

REINVENTING GOVERNMENT, P. 269

EXERCISE 25
TYPES OF
ORGANIZATIONS

Match the type of organization with its descriptive orientation and circle the category in which an entrepreneurial organization would fall.

| Power Orientation | | Exist simply to serve the needs of their members (for example, social groups) |

| Role Orientation | | Autocratic and hierarchical (for example, traditional businesses) |

| Task Orientation | | Extremely fluid and results oriented (for example, technology-oriented businesses) |

| Personal Orientation | | Carefully ordered by rules, procedures, and hierarchy (for example, bureaucracies) |

> "When organizations push authority into the hands of employees, they quickly discover that to get a handle on major problems or decisions, those employees need to work together in teams."
>
> —REINVENTING GOVERNMENT, P. 267

E X E R C I S E   2 6
STRENGTHS OF TEAMWORK

List the greatest strengths of teamwork organizations:

1.

2.

3.

What are teamwork's other strengths?

1.

2.

3.

4.

5.

On the following scale, indicate to what degree each question is true for your work environment (1 = not at all, 10 = very much) by placing a check mark in the appropriate box.

	1				5					10
1. Tasks and responsibilities are clearly organized.	☐	☐	☐	☐	☐	☐	☐	☐	☐	☐
2. People are trusted.	☐	☐	☐	☐	☐	☐	☐	☐	☐	☐
3. People are treated fairly.	☐	☐	☐	☐	☐	☐	☐	☐	☐	☐
4. Individual effort is rewarded appropriately.	☐	☐	☐	☐	☐	☐	☐	☐	☐	☐
5. People work together to solve problems.	☐	☐	☐	☐	☐	☐	☐	☐	☐	☐
6. People have a voice in decisions.	☐	☐	☐	☐	☐	☐	☐	☐	☐	☐
7. I understand *why* things are asked of me.	☐	☐	☐	☐	☐	☐	☐	☐	☐	☐
8. Red tape and procedures do not interfere with results.	☐	☐	☐	☐	☐	☐	☐	☐	☐	☐
9. Problems are shared.	☐	☐	☐	☐	☐	☐	☐	☐	☐	☐
10. I know what our mission is.	☐	☐	☐	☐	☐	☐	☐	☐	☐	☐
11. I know what our vision is.	☐	☐	☐	☐	☐	☐	☐	☐	☐	☐

METHOD 3: PROTECTING YOUR ENTREPRENEURS

To be successful, participatory organizations must not only empower employees and teams, but protect them. . . . Participatory management is also risky. It encourages employees to share information and confront underlying issues.

REINVENTING GOVERNMENT, P. 271

Example

Former Minnesota Governor Rudy Perpich created an initiative called Strive Toward Excellence in Performance (STEP) to empower and protect champions of change. The public-private STEP board, co-chaired by the governor, asked employees to submit proposals for team-based innovations, then gave the best ones their blessing and protection.

STEP did four things:

1. It gave people permission to innovate.

2. It offered them technical assistance.

3. It forced their bosses to sit up and listen.

4. It protected them when the inevitable flak hit.

The Perpich administration learned a number of valuable lessons from STEP:

1. Innovation often comes from the bottom up.

2. The Lone Ranger is not an appropriate role model. Projects run by teams do much better than those run by individuals.

3. Decentralization requires a firm commitment from the top.

METHOD 4: INVESTING IN THE EMPLOYEE

We found over and over again that entrepreneurial organizations paid their employees well and worked to improve the physical quality of their workplaces. In addition, they invested heavily in training.

REINVENTING GOVERNMENT, P. 275

EXERCISE 28
TRAINING SURVEY

By checking the appropriate box, indicate which training subjects you have taken or would like to take.

	Taken	Interested in Taking
1. Team Building	☐	☐
2. Meeting Skills	☐	☐
3. Leadership Skills	☐	☐
4. Empowerment	☐	☐
5. Reinventing Government Strategies	☐	☐
6. Change Management	☐	☐
7. Effective Writing Skills	☐	☐
8. Listening Skills	☐	☐
9. Coaching Skills	☐	☐

	Taken	*Interested in Taking*
10. Communication Skills	☐	☐
11. Time Management	☐	☐
12. Customer Service Skills	☐	☐
13. Creative Problem Solving	☐	☐
14. Supervisory Skills	☐	☐
15. Giving Corrective Feedback	☐	☐
16. Giving Positive Feedback	☐	☐
17. Computers	☐	☐
18. Developing Positive Assertiveness	☐	☐
19. Concentration Skills	☐	☐
20. Stress Management	☐	☐
21. Other_____	☐	☐
22. Other_____	☐	☐

PRINCIPLE VIII.

COMMUNITY-OWNED GOVERNMENT
EMPOWERING RATHER THAN SERVING

Before 1900, what little control existed over neighborhoods, health, education, and the like lay primarily with local communities, because so many products and services, whether public or private, were produced or sold locally. It was only with the emergence of an industrial economy of mass

production that we began to hire professionals and bureaucrats to do what families, neighborhoods, churches, and voluntary associations had done.

REINVENTING GOVERNMENT, P. 52

> **"We let bureaucrats control our public services, not those they intend to help. We rely on professionals to solve problems, not families and communities. We let the police, the doctors, the teachers, and the social workers have all the control, while the people they are serving have none. . . . We create dependency."**
>
> **REINVENTING GOVERNMENT, P. 51**

Shifting Your Locus of Control

Empower the most effective problem solvers by pulling ownership out of bureaucracy and into the community.

Definitions

Clients: "People who are dependent upon and controlled by their helpers and leaders. Clients are people who understand themselves in terms of their deficiencies and people who wait for others to act on their behalf.

Citizens: "People who understand their own problems in their own terms. Citizens perceive their relationship to one another and they believe in their capacity to act."

"Good clients make bad citizens.

Good citizens make strong communities."

—FORMER ST. PAUL MAYOR GEORGE LATIMER, 1986 "STATE OF THE CITY ADDRESS," QUOTED IN *REINVENTING GOVERNMENT*, P. 52

EXERCISE 29
BUREAUCRACY VS. COMMUNITY

List the services that were once locally owned but are now controlled by big government or big business.

1.

2.

3.

4.

5.

6.

7.

8.

9.

10.

COMMUNITY OWNERSHIP

> *"We must delight in each other, make others' condition our own, rejoice together, mourn together, labor and suffer together, always having before our eyes our community as members of the same body."*
>
> —JOHN WINTHROP, GOVERNOR OF THE MASSACHUSETTS BAY COLONY, 1630, IN M. SCOTT PECK, *THE DIFFERENT DRUM*, P. 26

Take Notes

Examples	Notes
Resettlement (Southeast Asia Refugee)	
Recycling (Seattle, Washington)	
Housing (Kenilworth-Parkside Public Housing Development)	

Examples	Notes
Education (Chicago, Illinois; New Haven, Connecticut)	
Home Instruction Program (Arkansas)	
Job Training	
Criminal Justice (San Francisco, California; Florida; Massachusetts; Philadelphia, Pennsylvania)	

PROFESSIONAL SERVICES VS. COMMUNITY CARE

Empowering communities not only changes expectations and instills confidence; it often provides far better solutions to problems than normal public services.

Contrast	*Example*
Communities have more commitment to their members than service delivery systems have to their clients.	
Communities understand their problems better than service professionals.	
Professionals and bureaucrats deliver services; communities solve problems.	

Contrast	Example
Communities focus on capacities; service systems focus on deficiencies.	
Institutions and professionals offer "service"; communities offer care.	
Communities are more flexible and creative than large service bureaucracies.	
Communities are cheaper than service professionals.	
Communities enforce standards of behavior more effectively than bureaucracies of service professionals.	

MODULE FOUR

INCREASING YOUR LEVERAGE

PRINCIPLE IX. **CATALYTIC GOVERNMENT**

PRINCIPLE X. **MARKET-ORIENTED GOVERNMENT**

PRINCIPLE IX.

CATALYTIC GOVERNMENT
STEERING RATHER THAN ROWING

[Entrepreneurial leaders] learned how to bring community groups and foundations together to build low-income housing; how to bring business, labor, and academia together to stimulate economic innovation and job creation; how to bring neighborhood groups and police together to solve the problems that underlay crime. In other words, they learned how to facilitate problem solving by catalyzing action throughout the community—how to steer rather than row.

REINVENTING GOVERNMENT, P. 28

Increasing Your Leverage

Uncouple steering and rowing, so you can use the best possible organizations—public, private, or nonprofit—to do the rowing.

Definitions

To govern: From a Greek word that means "helmsman," he or she who steers.

Steering: Setting policy, delivering funds to operational bodies (public and private), and evaluating performance. Requires people who see the entire universe of issues and possibilities and can balance competing demands for resources.

Rowing: Delivering services or enforcing compliance with rules. Should be done by separate staffs, each with its own mission and goals and its own sphere of action and autonomy. Requires people who focus intently on one mission and perform it well.

> *[The catalytic approach uses] "government for what it does best—raising resources and setting societal priorities through a democratic political process—while utilizing the private sector for what it does best—organizing the production of goods and services."*
>
> —LESTER M. SALAMON, *BEYOND PRIVATIZATION: THE TOOLS OF GOVERNMENT ACTION*, PP. 10–11

Examples

✔ *San Francisco, Boston,* and other cities pioneered "linkage" programs, in which corporations that wanted to construct buildings downtown had to provide quid pro quos, such as child care and low-income housing.

✔ *The California Department of Transportation* negotiated franchise agreements with four private consortia to build toll highways.

✔ *Massachusetts* boosted its funding of nongovernmental organizations to provide social services from $25 million in 1971 to $750 million—spread over 3,500 separate contracts and grants—in 1988.

ALTERNATIVES TO STANDARD SERVICE DELIVERY BY PUBLIC EMPLOYEES

Alternative	Example
A. Traditional	
1. Creating legal rules and sanctions	
2. Deregulation	
3. Monitoring and investigating	
4. Licensing	
5. Tax policy	
6. Grants	
7. Subsidies	
8. Loans	
9. Loan guarantees	
10. Contracting	

> *"Any attempt to combine governing with 'doing' on a large scale, paralyzes the decision-making capacity. Any attempt to have decision-making organs actually 'do,' also means very poor 'doing.' They are not focused on 'doing.' They are not equipped for it. They are not fundamentally concerned with it."*
>
> —PETER F. DRUCKER, *THE AGE OF DISCONTINUITY*, P. 233

Alternative	*Example*
B. Innovative	
11. Franchising	
12. Public-private partnerships	
13. Public-public partnerships	
14. Quasi-public corporations	
15. Public enterprise	
16. Procurement	
17. Insurance	
18. Rewards, awards, and bounties	
19. Changing public investment policy	

> *"If corporations are to succeed in today's supercompetitive global market, they need the highest quality 'inputs' they can get—the most knowledgeable workers, the most groundbreaking research, the cheapest capital, the best infrastructure. This makes government's various roles as educator, trainer, research funder, regulator, rule setter, and infrastructure operator far more important than they were thirty years ago."*
>
> —*Reinventing Government*, p. 33

Alternative	*Example*
B. Innovative	
20. Technical assistance	
21. Information	
22. Referral	
23. Volunteers	
24. Vouchers	
25. Impact fees	
26. Catalyzing nongovernmental efforts	
27. Convening nongovernmental leaders	
28. Jawboning	

Alternative	Example
C. Avant-Garde	
29. Seed money	
30. Equity investments	
31. Voluntary associations	
32. Coproduction or self-help	
33. Quid pro quos	
34. Demand management	
35. Sale, exchange, or use of property	
36. Restructuring the market	

PUBLIC SECTOR, PRIVATE SECTOR, OR THIRD SECTOR

> *"Services can be contracted out or turned over to the private sector. But governance cannot. We can privatize discrete steering functions, but not the overall process of governance. If we did, we would have no mechanism by which to make collective decisions, no way to set the rules of the marketplace, no means to enforce rules of behavior. We would lose all sense of equity and altruism: services that could not generate a profit, whether housing for the homeless or health care for the poor, would barely exist. Third sector organizations could never shoulder the entire load."*
>
> —REINVENTING GOVERNMENT, P. 45

Definitions

Public sector:

Publicly owned and democratically controlled; exists to meet public or societal needs.

Private sector:

Privately owned and controlled; exists to accumulate private profit.

Third sector:

Privately owned and controlled; exists to meet public or social needs, not to accumulate private wealth.

EXERCISE 32
QUALITIES DESIRED IN SERVICE PROVIDERS

Rate the degree of each quality offered by each sector (H = high; L = low; M = moderate)

Sector Qualities	*Public*	*Private*	*Third*
Public Sector Strengths:			
• Stability			
• Ability to handle issues outside central mission			
• Immunity to favoritism			
Private Sector Strengths:			
• Ability to respond to rapidly changing conditions			
• Ability to innovate			
• Tendency to replicate success			
• Tendency to abandon the obsolete or failed			
• Willingness to take risks			
• Ability to generate capital			
• Professional expertise			
• Ability to capture economies of scale			
Third Sector Strengths:			
• Ability to reach diverse populations			
• Compassion and commitment			
• Holistic treatment of problems			
• Ability to generate trust			

TASKS BEST SUITED TO EACH SECTOR

Indicate with a check mark which sector is best suited for each task.

Tasks	Public	Private	Third
1. Policy management			
2. Economic tasks			
3. Social tasks			
4. Regulation			
5. Investment tasks			
6. Tasks that require volunteer labor			
7. Enforcement of equity			
8. Profit generation			
9. Tasks that generate little profit			
10. Prevention of discrimination			
11. Promotion of self-sufficiency			
12. Promotion of individual responsibility			
13. Prevention of exploitation			
14. Promotion of community			
15. Promotion of social cohesion			
16. Promotion of commitment to welfare of others			

STEERING ORGANIZATIONS

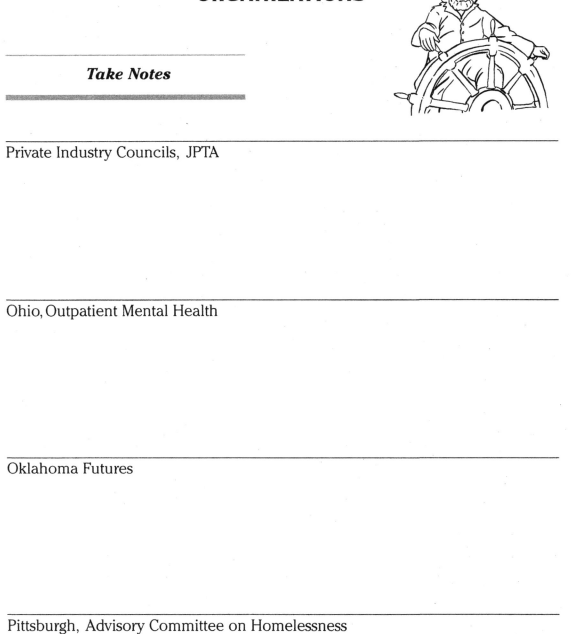

Private Industry Councils, JPTA

Ohio, Outpatient Mental Health

Oklahoma Futures

Pittsburgh, Advisory Committee on Homelessness

MARKET-ORIENTED GOVERNMENT
LEVERAGING CHANGE THROUGH THE MARKET

Structuring the market ... is a way of using public leverage to shape private decisions to achieve collective goals. It is a classic method of entrepreneurial governance: active government without bureaucratic government.

REINVENTING GOVERNMENT, P. 284

Increasing Your Leverage

Rather than creating public organizations, create incentives that move people in the direction in which the community wants to go.

Examples

✔ ***Mortgages:*** The Federal Housing Administration (FHA) pioneered a new form of mortgage, which required only 20 percent down and let the borrower repay over 30 years.

✔ ***"Bottle Bills":*** Rather than creating elaborate and expensive recycling programs, some states have simply required buyers to pay five-cent deposits on each bottle or can—to be refunded when the bottle or can is returned.

✔ ***Child care:*** Rather than funding public day care facilities, some governments provide tax credits or vouchers for low-income families.

E X E R C I S E   3 4
PROGRAMS

Indicate whether the statements below are true **(T)** or false **(F)**.

T   **F**   **1.** Programs are driven by constituencies, not by customers.

T   **F**   **2.** Programs are driven by politics, not by policy.

T   **F**   **3.** Programs create "turf," which public agencies defend at all costs.

T   **F**   **4.** Programs tend to create fragmented service delivery systems.

T   **F**   **5.** Programs are not self-correcting.

T   **F**   **6.** Programs rarely die.

T   **F**   **7.** Programs rarely achieve the scale necessary to have a significant impact.

T   **F**   **8.** Programs normally use commands, not incentives.

> *"Programs tend to be created in response to a constituency group–defined claim on resources, not in response to demand from individuals or labor markets. . . . The distribution of things provided by government responds to their supply, not to the demand for them by individuals."*
>
> PHILIP POWER AND JAN URBAN-LURAIN,
> *CREATING A HUMAN INVESTMENT SYSTEM*, PP. 4–5

COMMAND-AND-CONTROL DRAWBACKS

EXERCISE 35
COMMAND-AND-CONTROL REGULATION

Indicate whether the statements below are true **(T)** or false **(F)**.

T   F   1. Command-and-control strategies do not change the underlying economic incentives that drive firms or individuals.

T   F   2. Command-and-control strategies rely on the threat of penalties— but in a political environment, many of those penalties can never be assessed.

T   F   3. Command-and-control regulation is a very slow process.

T   F   4. Regulations that specify the exact technology that industry must use to control pollution discourage technological innovation.

T   F   5. Command-and-control approaches are extremely expensive.

T   F   6. Command-and-control regulation has a tendency to focus on symptoms rather than on causes.

> *"A great deal of time and money goes into fighting and circumventing regulations, and illegal dumping increases."*
>
> —REINVENTING GOVERNMENT, P. **300**

WHAT IT TAKES TO MAKE
A MARKET WORK

Select the elements needed for an effective and fair market.

☐ Supply

☐ Demand

☐ Government programs

☐ Strong command-and-control mechanisms

☐ Accessibility

☐ Information

☐ Rules

☐ Policing

☐ Freedom from monitoring

☐ Minimal information to eliminate confusion

☐ Only one service provider to minimize the decision-making process

> *"Some markets are deeply flawed. When a small number of firms dominate a market, true competition often disappears. When customers do not have adequate information, they are often victimized."*
>
> —*REINVENTING GOVERNMENT,* P. **291**

HOW GOVERNMENTS ARE RESTRUCTURING THE MARKETPLACE

Markets are to social and economic activity what computers are to information: using prices as their primary mechanism, they send and receive signals almost instantaneously, processing millions of inputs efficiently and allowing millions of people to make decisions for themselves.

REINVENTING GOVERNMENT, P. 285

E X E R C I S E 3 7
MARKETPLACE

Methods	Examples
Setting the rules of the marketplace	
Providing information to consumers	
Creating or augmenting demand	
Catalyzing private sector suppliers	
Creating institutions to fill gaps in the market	

> *"Market mechanisms have many advantages over administrative mechanisms. . . . Markets are decentralized; they are (normally) competitive; they empower customers to make choices; and they link resources directly to results. Markets also respond quickly to rapid change. And . . . market restructuring allows government to achieve the scale necessary to solve serious problems."*
>
> —*REINVENTING GOVERNMENT*, P. 284

Methods	Examples
Catalyzing the formation of new market sectors	
Sharing the risk of expanding supply with the private sector	
Changing public investment policy	
Acting as a broker for buyers and sellers	
Pricing activities through the tax code	
Pricing activities through impact fees	
Managing demand through user fees	
Building community	

1. If water consumption were too high, what would you recommend to the city council to solve the problem?

2. How would you encourage a community to use more recycled materials and equipment?

3. How could "smart cards"—plastic cards that can store information on embedded computer chips—be used to change public systems like health care, food stamps, education, and training?

BECOME AN ACTIVE MEMBER IN THE MOVEMENT TO BANISH BUREAUCRACY—

Join the Alliance for Redesigning Government!

Cofounded by David Osborne in 1993, the Alliance exists to bring change agents together to share ideas, concerns, and practices. Since its inception, the Alliance has developed a number of resources to support you as a change agent fighting to create 21st-century government.

★ *The Public Innovator* magazine—The latest news on efforts to redesign government—at local, state, and federal levels.

★ *The Public Innovator* Learning Network—Our extensive Web site features case studies from all areas of reinvention and links to other sites of interest.

★ Design Labs—In-depth projects that bring together teams of practitioners and experts to create, test, refine, and implement new approaches.

★ Conferences—Our conferences provide you with practical and usable tools for your reinvention efforts, plus the opportunity to network with others in the reinvention arena.

★ And much more to come!

Whether you are on the front lines of government reinvention or a citizen interested in learning how government can become more effective, the Alliance can provide you with the information you need to understand the process; the tools you need to make a difference!

To join this proactive network for government change, simply complete the card below and fax or mail it to us. Our fax number is (202) 347-3252.

✔ I need to know more about the Alliance and its activities.

Please send the information I have requested below.

☐ General information on the Alliance   ☐ Upcoming conferences
☐ *The Public Innovator* Learning Network   ☐ Membership
☐ FREE issues of *The Public Innovator*   ☐ Design Labs

NAME _____ PHONE ( ) _____

ORGANIZATION _____

ADDRESS _____

CITY _____ STATE _____ ZIP _____

◢LLIANCE FOR REDESIGNING GOVERNMENT
National Academy of Public Administration

SEE WHAT OTHER INNOVATORS HAVE BEEN DOING—

Visit the Alliance's Web site

Information on the Alliance activities, case studies, links to other sites of interest to innovators—you'll find all this and more at:

http://www.alliance.napawash.org

Stop by today or e-mail us at:

innovate@napawash.org

If the card is missing, call (202) 466-6887 or send your name and address to:

The Alliance for Redesigning Government

1120 G Street, NW

Suite 850

Washington DC 20005

SERIOUS ABOUT REINVENTING?

Are you serious about banishing bureaucracy from your organization but not quite sure where to start? No matter where you are in the process of reinventing your organization, The Public Strategies Group can provide you with tools to further implement the five C's in your organization.

The principals of the Public Strategies Group, who include author David Osborne, have experienced firsthand the challenges of implementing fundamental change in public sector organizations. We have succeeded enough to know it can be done and failed enough to have learned a great deal about it.

The Public Strategies Group (PSG) is an enterprise comprised of some of this country's most advanced thinkers and practitioners of post-bureaucratic government. Together with its consortium of innovative public sector consultants called the Reinventing Government Network, PSG helps public agencies transform themselves into customer-focused, results-driven enterprises. We work primarily with public sector organizations. Our vision is a public sector that delights its customers with outstanding service at a reasonable price.

Please contact us:

The Public Strategies Group, Inc.

http://www.psgrp.com

(612) 227-9774

reinvent@psgrp.com

NOTES

NOTES

NOTES

NOTES

NOTES